Fuck
You

POCKET TRANSLATOR

Published and distributed by Knock Knock
6080 Center Drive
Los Angeles, CA 90045
knockknockstuff.com
Knock Knock is a registered trademark of
Knock Knock LLC

This book is a work of humor meant solely for enter-
tainment purposes. In no event will Knock Knock
be liable to any reader for any damages, including
direct, indirect, incidental, special, consequential,
or punitive damages, arising out of or in connection
with the use of the information contained in this
book. So there.

ISBN: 978-168349186-6
UPC: 825703-50304-3

10 9 8 7 6 5 4 3 2 1

POCKET TRANSLATOR

A Strongly Worded Lexicon

INTRODUCTION

Life on Earth is full of F-bomb moments and awful people, and this book is filled with ways to express your true feelings about them. Compiled with a far-flung team of linguistic consultants from Dubai to Shanghai, the *Fuck You Pocket Translator* will enable you to express your outrage with international flair. All major world languages are included, as well as numerous smaller languages. Just for fun, we've also included a few fictional idioms. Best of all, each phrase is presented with easy-to-follow phonetic pronunciation, as well as a map to indicate the countries where it is most commonly spoken.

Be prepared: as you travel the world, it is entirely possible that you will meet a few rotten eggs. Travel is well known to improve people's moods, but everyone has bad days.

Of course, as a visitor to a foreign land, you must strive to control your temper, go with the flow, and respect local cultures. Sounds obvious, but before you get on that plane, do a quick search of a country's general laws and avoid foolish missteps.

This holds true even when you're not upset. Indeed, it's easy to offend people of other cultures without any ill intent whatsoever. "All the rules change when you're in another country," warns Sheryl Hill, executive director of Depart Smart, a nonprofit dedicated to improving travel safety. One famous example of cultural misunderstanding occurred in 1985 in Rome. Five Americans were arrested outside the Vatican for making the signature gesture of the Texas Longhorn football team. This gesture—a clenched fist with the index finger and little finger extended, is a highly obscene gesture in Italy. "When traveling abroad, make sure you understand the local laws and regulations," Hill recommends.

With this sage advice in mind, you'll be free to venture forth into the wide world of human emotion. Besides phrases, this book provides useful tips and fascinating insights about expletives and F-word equivalents around the world—like who's said "fuck" on live TV, and how to insult people without uttering a word.

You're a worldly person. You're an expressive person. The *Fuck You Pocket Translator* will provoke and inspire the highly irreverent globetrotter inside you—whether or not you ever leave home.

103 LANGUAGES

Afrikaans	Dutch	Hmong
Akan	Elvish	Hungarian
Albanian	Esperanto	Icelandic
Amharic	Estonian	Igbo
Arabic	Farsi	Indonesian
Armenian	Finnish	Irish
Asturian	Flemish	Italian
Azerbaijani	French	Jamaican
Basque	Galician	Japanese
Belarusian	Georgian	Javanese
Bemba	German	Kannada
Bengali	Greek	Kazakh
Bulgarian	Guarani	Khmer
Burmese	Haitian	Kinyarwanda
Cantonese	Hausa	Kirundi
Catalan	Hebrew	Klingon
Chewa	High	Korean
Czech	Valyrian	Ladino
Danish	Hindi	Lao

Latvian	Russian	Welsh
Lithuanian	Serbian	Xhosa
Lombard	Sinhala	Yiddish
Macedonian	Slovak	Yoruba
Malagasy	Slovenian	Zulu
Malay	Somali	
Maltese	Spanish	
Mandarin	Sundanese	
Maori	Swahili	
Marshallese	Swedish	
Moldovan	Tagalog	
Mongolian	Tajik	
Nepali	Tamil	
Norwegian	Thai	
Oromo	Tigrinya	
Pashto	Tonga	
Pig Latin	Turkish	
Polish	Ukrainian	
Portuguese	Urdu	
Punjabi	Uzbek	
Romanian	Vietnamese	

Fok jou

(fuck you)

Wo twɛ asere

(wutch-weh ah-sih-rih)

Note: Akan is a tonal language and does not stress syllables.

COUNTRIES SPOKEN IN:

Côte d'Ivoire (Ivory Coast), Ghana

Të qifsha

(tuh **keef**-shah)

COUNTRIES SPOKEN IN:

Albania, Italy, Kosovo, Macedonia, Montenegro,
Serbia

Female recipient:

ተበጅ

(teh-beh-**jigh**)

Male recipient:

ተበዳ

(teh-beh-**dah**)

COUNTRIES SPOKEN IN:

Ethiopia

Male recipient:

تباً لكَ

(tabb-**bahn** laka)

Female recipient:

تباً لكِ

(tabb-**bahn** lakee)

COUNTRIES SPOKEN IN:

Algeria, Bahrain, Chad, Comoros, Djibouti, Egypt, Iraq, Israel, Jordan, Kuwait, Lebanon, Libya, Mali, Mauritania, Morocco, Niger, Oman, Palestine, Qatar, Saudi Arabia, Somalia, Sudan, Syria, Tanzania, Tunisia, Turkey, United Arab Emirates, Yemen

մինետ ձեզ

(minet dzez)

COUNTRIES SPOKEN IN:

Armenia, Georgia, Iran, Lebanon, Russia,
Turkey, Ukraine

Que te fodan

(keh teh **foh**-dan)

COUNTRIES SPOKEN IN:

Spain

Siktir

(seek-teer)

COUNTRIES SPOKEN IN:

Republic of Azerbaijan, Georgia, Iran, Iraq,
Russia, Turkey

ACTIONS SWEAR LOUDER THAN WORDS

The middle finger may be the most popular gesticular insult in Western culture, but other actions can deliver equal offense. For instance, exposing the bottom of your shoe to another person is a serious insult in Muslim, Hindu, and Buddhist countries. Other widely offensive acts:

- **"The moutza":** A traditional Greek put-down made by stretching your hand open and thrusting it forward. It symbolizes rubbing waste (including the human kind) into the recipient's face.

- **Bras d'honneur:** A Western European favorite. One arm is L-shaped, with its fist pointing upward, while the other hand slaps or grips the bent arm's bicep. This gesture translates to "arm of honor" in French and signifies "up yours."

- **Two-fingered salute:** A peace sign in the U.S. may be amicable but in reverse (with knuckles forward), it's seen as derogatory in the UK, Australia, and New Zealand.

Zoaz popatik hartzera

(soh-as poh-pah-teek art-zay-rah)

COUNTRIES SPOKEN IN:

Spain, France

Пайшоў на хуй

(pai-show na khuy)

COUNTRIES SPOKEN IN:

Belarus, Latvia, Lithuania, Poland, Russia,
Ukraine

We mbwa we

(weh em-bwah weh)

Zambia, Democratic Republic of the Congo, Tanzania

দূর হও

(dur ho)

Майната ти

(my-nah-tah tee)

COUNTRIES SPOKEN IN:

Bulgaria, Albania, Greece, Macedonia,
Romania, Serbia, Turkey, Ukraine

(naar low mah tar)

Note: Tones in Burmese are flat, therefore no
syllables are stressed.

COUNTRIES SPOKEN IN:

Myanmar

屌你

(dee-yu nay)

Que et fotin

(cat-**fo**-teen)

F-BOMB ORIGINS

Thank the Germanic peoples for bringing "fuck" into existence. According to scholars, the f-word has similarities to the German word for fornicating, *ficken*, the Middle Dutch's *fokken*, meaning "to breed," and the Norwegian regional *fukka*—which means sexual intercourse. Etymologists believe "fuck" emerged into the English language during the fourteenth century, although the word's progression in vernacular to "fuck you" continues to be debated. However, the idea that "fuck you" derived from the Hundred Years' War is fake folklore. As the tale goes, the English yelled "pluck yew" (the action of drawing an English longbow) at the French upon the former's victory during the Battle of Agincourt. In reality, in 1996 the NPR show *Car Talk* shared this story in a joke segment and gullible internet users continued to spread it. It would be hard to imagine Joan of Arc being on the receiving end of a royal "pluck yew."

Chakuti chako

(chah-koo-tee-chah-koh)

COUNTRIES SPOKEN IN:

Malawi, Mozambique, Zambia, Zimbabwe

Jdi do prdele

(yee-**dyee** doh **per**-deh-leh)

COUNTRIES SPOKEN IN:

Czech Republic

Fuck dig

(fuck daee)

Je kan de pot op

(yuh kan deh **pot** op)

COUNTRIES SPOKEN IN:
The Netherlands, Belgium, Suriname, Aruba,
Curaçao, France, Sint Maarten

Ego

(ee-goh)

COUNTRIES SPOKEN IN:

Rivendell and Lothlorien, in J. R. R. Tolkien's
Middle-earth.

Forfikiĝu

(for-fee-**kee**-joo)

COUNTRIES SPOKEN IN:

China, Korea, Japan, Iran, Brazil, Argentina, Mexico, Togo

Mine persse

(mee-ne **per**-seh)

لعنت به تو

(lah-**naat** beh toh)

COUNTRIES SPOKEN IN:

Iran, Afghanistan, Tajikistan, Uzbekistan

Haista vittu

(high-sta veet-too)

Rot op

(rote ohp)

COUNTRIES SPOKEN IN:
Belgium, France, the Netherlands

MICHELANGELO AND HIS SISTINE "FUCK YOU"

Artists Botticelli and Michelangelo hid insults in their Sistine Chapel artworks, aiming them at the notorious Della Rovere family (whose name translates to "of the oak tree"). This clan produced not one but two popes: Sixtus IV, who built the Sistine Chapel in his own name, and Julius II, Sixtus' unpleasant nephew. According to Vatican docent Roy Doliner, Botticelli used his Sistine panel to portray Satan jumping into an oak tree, symbolizing the devil's relation to the Della Rovere family. On Michelangelo's revered ceiling, Pope Julius is portrayed as the prophet Zechariah, with a cherub on his shoulder. But close observers will note, the cherub is making a hand gesture known as the "fig," or *fica*: a clenched fist with the thumb tucked between the forefinger and middle finger. The fig has a variety of meanings, including female genitalia. In this instance, it meant something akin to "screw you." Or should we say "fig you"?

Va te faire foutre

(vah teh fair **fou**-treuh)

COUNTRIES SPOKEN IN:

France, Belgium, Benin, Burkina Faso, Burundi, Cameroon, Canada, Central African Republic, Chad, Comoros, Côte d'Ivoire (Ivory Coast), Djibouti, Dominica, Equatorial Guinea, Gabon, Guinea, Haiti, Luxembourg, Madagascar, Mali, Monaco, Niger, Democratic Republic of the Congo, Republic of Congo, Rwanda, Santa Lucia, Senegal, Seychelles, Switzerland, Togo, Vanuatu

Que che fodan

(ke cheh **foh**-dan)

შენი დედა ვატირე

(sheni **deh-dah** vuh-tyre)

COUNTRIES SPOKEN IN:

Georgia

Fick Dich

(fick dish)

COUNTRIES SPOKEN IN:

Austria, Belgium, Germany, Liechtenstein,
Luxembourg, Switzerland

Άντε γαμήσου

(an-te gam-**ee**-sou)

COUNTRIES SPOKEN IN:

Cyprus, Greece

Yapiro

(ee-ah-pee-ro)

COUNTRIES SPOKEN IN:

Paraguay, Argentina, Brazil, Bolivia

Koulangèt manman w

(kool-ah-**geht** mah-**mahw**)

COUNTRIES SPOKEN IN:
Haiti

Kaniyar ka

(kah-nee-yar kah)

LIVE FROM NEW YORK, IT'S SATURDAY NIGHT—FUCK!

Live television has proven to be a great source of unexpected F-bombs (known as "fleeting expletives" in broadcast law). In 1965, Kenneth Tynan, director of England's National Theater, dropped the first on-air "fuck" in Britain during BBC's satirical talk show *BBC-3*. Nearly a decade later, Sex Pistols guitarist Steve Jones called talk show host Bill Grundy a "fucking rotter" after Grundy hit on fellow guest Siouxsie Sioux, a friend of the Pistols. In the U.S., late-night variety show *Saturday Night Live* has been peppered with unfiltered "fucks" throughout its history. Stars who have uttered the four-letter word live include hosts Samuel L. Jackson and Kristen Stewart, musical guest Prince, and cast member Jenny Slate (whose SNL contract was not renewed after her slipup). At least those celebrities, in terms of comedy, really *did* give a fuck.

לך תזדיין

(lekh tiz-**dah**-yin)

Ifas maisi yeri

(iff-ahhs may-see yare-ee)

COUNTRIES SPOKEN IN:

In *Game of Thrones*, the continent of Essos, Valyria (now gone)

भाड़ में जाओ

(baad may jow)

Ua koj

(wah kaw)

COUNTRIES SPOKEN IN:
China, Vietnam, Laos, Myanmar, Thailand

Cseszd meg

(chezd meg)

COUNTRIES SPOKEN IN:

Hungary

Farðu í rassgat

(far-thee rus-cut)

COUNTRIES SPOKEN IN:
Iceland

Gaa n'ime òkù mmụọ nwụọ

(gaa-nah-**ih-meh** oh-koo mm-moo-ooh nooh-ooh)

Sialan kau

(see-ah-**lund** kau)

COUNTRIES SPOKEN IN:

Indonesia

Gabh suas ort féin

(gow **su**-is urt hayn)

COUNTRIES SPOKEN IN:

Ireland

Vaffanculo

(va-fan-koo-lo)

COUNTRIES SPOKEN IN:
Italy, Switzerland, Vatican City

BITTER SWEARS TO SWALLOW

When insulting others, typical targets include an adversary's intelligence, or his mother. But in some places, insulting a person's health can be just as devastating. According to the BBC, ridiculing an individual's physical well-being seems to upset the Dutch more than criticizing his or her morals. Popular affronts include straight-to-the-point insults like *tyfus* ("tuberculosis") and *poke* ("smallpox"). *Kanker* ("cancer") has also become a go-to interjection, comparable to "damn it," which may be combined with other insults to deliver a powerful one-two punch—say, *kankerlul* ("cancer dick"). An ill-willed exclamation from Poland is *cholera*—which more or less wishes bacterial disease upon its recipient. And then there's always the more-direct English route: simply tell someone to "drop dead."

Suck yu madda

(suck yu maw-da)

COUNTRIES SPOKEN IN:

Jamaica

ばか野郎

(ba-ka ya-ro)

Diancuk sampeyan

(dee-an-chook sum-pee-en)

COUNTRIES SPOKEN IN:

Indonesia, Suriname

ತೊಲಗು ಇಲ್ಲಿಂದ

(toh-la-**goo** ill-in-dah)

Кетші бар

(ket-chee bahr)

COUNTRIES SPOKEN IN:

Kazakhstan

ចុយម្រាយ

(choy mray)

Note: Tones in Khmer are flat, therefore no syllables are stressed.

COUNTRIES SPOKEN IN:

Cambodia

Gaswere

(gah-skwe-reh)

COUNTRIES SPOKEN IN:

Rwanda

Iskwere

(ice-koo-weh-re)

COUNTRIES SPOKEN IN:

Burundi

SHORTEN YOUR SWEARS

With the rise of text messaging, profanity has become easier (and more abbreviated) than ever. Dig into internet trolls or spice up your texts with these foul-mouthed acronyms:

FO: Fuck Off

FOAD: Fuck Off and Die

FYFI: For Your Fucking Information

GAGF: Go and Get Fucked

GFY: Go Fuck Yourself

BFD: Big Fucking Deal

IHTFP: I Hate This Fucking Place

GTFO: Get the Fuck Out

IDGAF: I Don't Give a Fuck

DILLIGAF: Do I Look Like I Give A Fuck

NMFP: Not My Fucking Problem

STFU: Shut the Fuck Up

AMF: Adios Mother Fucker

TARFU: Things Are Really Fucked Up

WOFTAM: Waste of Fucking Time and Money

QI'yaH soH

(kee-yah shokh)

COUNTRIES SPOKEN IN:

Star Trek's Klingon Empire

꺼져 이 새끼야

(koh-juh ee say-kee-ya)

COUNTRIES SPOKEN IN:

South Korea, North Korea

לְבַאיי

(Yy oby)

ສິ້ເເໜ້ມຶງ

(see my mung)

COUNTRIES SPOKEN IN:

Laos, Thailand

Ej Dirst!

(ayy deerst)

Eik po velnių

(aik po **vel**-nyu)

COUNTRIES SPOKEN IN:

Lithuania

Va' a da via el cùu

(va rah **vee**-ah all koo)

Еби се

(eh-bee se)

Ndàna mandeha any

(ndah-nah mann-deh ah-nee)

Pukimak

(poo-key-muck)

COUNTRIES SPOKEN IN:

Malaysia, Brunei, Indonesia, Singapore

INSULT WITH INCISIVENESS

When a simple "fuck you" isn't enough, take a page from these put-down masters:

- **Shakespearean Barbs:** Craft your own Shakespearean put-downs using this fool-proof formula: first, choose a degrading adjective; next, a verb-derived adjective; and finally, link them with a rich noun (for example, "poisonous bunch-backed toad!").

- **Joan River Jeers:** Rivers' crass jibes left a memorable sting. To offend like Joan: mask your insult with praise, then take a stab at your target's character (for example, "Marie Osmond is so pure, not even Moses could part her knees.").

- **Trash Like Triumph:** Conan O'Brien's favorite puppet, Triumph the Insult Comic Dog, roasts people at public events and with a cigar in his mouth to boot. To mimic Triumph's style: interrupt, then state the obvious (for example, "Pardon me, I only know your basic French expressions like 'I surrender.'").

Mur ħudu f'sormok

(murr **hoo**-doof-sore-mok)

COUNTRIES SPOKEN IN:

Malta

操你妈

(tsao nee mah)

Pōkōkōhua

(poh-koh-koh-**hoo**-a)

COUNTRIES SPOKEN IN:

New Zealand, Cook Islands

Kwele eōṃ

(kweh-leh eh-um)

COUNTRIES SPOKEN IN:

Marshall Islands

Du-te naibii!

(doo-tay nigh-bee)

COUNTRIES SPOKEN IN:

Moldova

Шаа

(shaah)

COUNTRIES SPOKEN IN:

Mongolia

म तिमीलाई घृणा गर्छु

(mah tim-ee-lai
green-ah gar-choo)

COUNTRIES SPOKEN IN:

Nepal

Faen ta deg

(faan ta dehy)

SHIP THE SHIT

When words aren't enough, a surprise gift to your adversary can do all the talking for you. Glitter bombs consist of parcels jam-packed with spring-loaded sparkles—which rain down upon the recipient upon opening, and subsequently get stuck *everywhere* (hair, clothes, rugs, pets). Another stealthy mail-order gift: a brick. Since throwing a brick at your enemy's window is technically vandalism, this option is worth pursuing.

Finally, if you want to go the extreme route, you can send your target a bag of animal excrement. No joke: there's an online company, touting itself as "a professional poop delivery service," that allows shoppers to order and send stool to unsuspecting recipients. All feces are from the bowels of farm animals, including cows, horses, pigs, goats, or chickens—customer's pick. Gives new meaning to "junk mail," doesn't it?

Sii salee

(see-sah-lee)

و دی غیم

(wah dee gha-yem)

COUNTRIES SPOKEN IN:

Afghanistan, Pakistan

Uckfay ouyay

(uck-fay ooh-yay)

Pieprz się

(**peep** shee-yeh)

COUNTRIES SPOKEN IN:

Poland

Vai se foder

(vye see foo-**day**)

COUNTRIES SPOKEN IN:

Portugal, Brazil, Angola, Cape Verde, East Timor, Macau, Guinea-Bissau, Mozambique, São Tomé and Príncipe

ਬੁੰਡ ਮਰਾ

(boon'd mraa)

COUNTRIES SPOKEN IN:

India, Pakistan

Dă-te în pula mea

(**daa**-teh in **poo**-la meah)

Пошел на хуй

(**pah**-shol nah **hoo**-ee)

Russia, Belarus, Kazakhstan, Ukraine

Jebi se

(yeh-bee seh)

උඹ පලයන් බං

(oom-bah pah-lah-yan bahm)

COUNTRIES SPOKEN IN:
Sri Lanka

JUST WHAT THE DOCTOR ORDERED

Cursing can actually do the body good. Research has shown that swearing can reduce pain, increase circulation, elevate endorphins, and provide "an overall sense of calm, control, and well-being," according to *Psychology Today*. Another study by the UK's Keele University suggests that swearing improves pain tolerance, triggering the brain's amygdala—the part of the limbic system that processes emotional reactions, memory, and judgment. When one curses due to sudden pain, the amygdala boosts the body's stamina to help relieve discomfort. Other academic findings suggest that cursing is a successful coping mechanism for anger and helps reduce pent-up aggression. Verbal outbursts act as a warning to back off, similar to a cat's hiss. Clearly, strong language is strong medicine, and should be indulged in as frequently as possible for proper mental hygiene.

Choď do riti

(hodj doh ree-tee)

COUNTRIES SPOKEN IN:

Slovakia

Jebi se

(yeh-bee seh)

COUNTRIES SPOKEN IN:

Slovenia

Anaa ku waso

(ana-ˈku-**waas**-oh)

Note: Apostrophes represent a scratchy "krr"
throat sound vibrating at the top and
back of the mouth.

COUNTRIES SPOKEN IN:

Somalia, Dijibouti, Ethiopia

Jódete

(hoh-deh-teh)

COUNTRIES SPOKEN IN:

Argentina, Bolivia, Colombia, Chile, Costa Rica,
Cuba, Dominican Republic, Ecuador, Equatorial
Guinea, El Salvador, Guatemala, Honduras,
Mexico, Nicaragua, Panama, Paraguay, Peru,
Puerto Rico, Uruguay, Venezuela, Spain

Bangsat nu

(baang saat nu)

COUNTRIES SPOKEN IN:

Indonesia

Unatiwa

(ooh-nah-tee-wah)

Dra åt helvete

(draw **oat** hell-vay-ta)

COUNTRIES SPOKEN IN:

Sweden, Finland

Puta ka

(poo-ta kah)

COUNTRIES SPOKEN IN:

Philippines

LOST IN TRANSLATION

Hatred is a universal emotion, and its expression is infinitely varied. These zingers don't sound bad in English, but they have great heft in their respective languages:

- Amharic: *Silbabot*. Literal translation: "You are the fatty layer on my warm milk." Actual meaning: "You are annoying."

- Québécois French: *Tabernacle*. Literal translation: "The altar." Actual meaning: "fuck."

- Arabic: *Teezak hamra*. Literal translation: "Your butt is red (like a monkey's)!" Actual meaning: "You're a dummy."

- Mandarin: *Hún dàn*. Literal translation: "Mixed egg." Actual meaning: "You bastard."

- Japanese: 豆腐の角に頭をぶつけて死ね (*Tofu no kado ni atama wo butsukete shine*): Literal translation: "Hit your head on a corner of tofu and die!" Actual meaning: "You're a complete idiot."

- Yiddish: *Gey kakken oifen ya*. Literal translation: "Go take a poop in the sea." Actual meaning: "Go to hell."

Дафъ шав

(dahf shahv)

COUNTRIES SPOKEN IN:

Tajikistan, Uzbekistan

ஒத்தா

(oh-ta)

COUNTRIES SPOKEN IN:

India, Sri Lanka

ไปตายซะ

(pay tai sah)

Male recipient:

ተረዋእ

(teh-reh-wa-ah)

Female recipient:

ተረውኢ

(teh-reh way-ee)

COUNTRIES SPOKEN IN:

Eritrea, Ethiopia

Fule'i
(foo-lay-ee)

Siktir git

(**seek**-teer geet)

COUNTRIES SPOKEN IN:

Turkey, Cyprus, Northern Cyprus

Пішов ти

(pee-shov tee)

بھاڑ میں جاؤ
(bhaad main jao)

COUNTRIES SPOKEN IN:

Pakistan, India

Seni sikaman

(seh-nee see-kah-mahn)

COUNTRIES SPOKEN IN:

Uzbekistan

Địt mẹ mày

(dit meh my)

COUNTRIES SPOKEN IN:

Vietnam

CINEMATIC CENSURING

What's the cost of cursing on American TV? The FCC changed the fine for obscenities on network television from $32,500 to $325,000 in 2005. While shows have been able to maneuver around this censorship and build actual fan-favorite euphemisms, including *Battlestar Galactica*'s "frak," *Farscape*'s "frell," and *The Good Place*'s "fork," altering movie dialogue to fit small-screen standards is more challenging. Take, for instance, the following edited-for-TV movie quotes:

- **Snakes on a Plane**: "I have had it with these monkey-fighting snakes on this Monday-to-Friday plane!"

- **The Usual Suspects**: "Hand me the keys, you fairy godmother."

- **Jackie Brown**: "Freeze, moldy fingers!"

- **Die Hard**: "Yippee-ki-yay, Mr. Falcon!"

- **Basic Instinct**: "I wasn't dating him. I was having sex with him."

- **The Big Lebowski**: "See what happens when you find a stranger in the alps?"

Twll dy dîn di Ffaro

(tool duh dean dee **farr**-ohh)

COUNTRIES SPOKEN IN:

Wales

Ubatyiwe

(oo-bah-chee-way)

אי קוש מיר אין תחת

(kush meer in tuh-khes)

COUNTRIES SPOKEN IN:

Israel, United States

Dó ẹ

(doh-eh)

Fusegi

(feh-ooh-**see**-gee)

LANGUAGES BY REGION

A geographic breakdown of where this book's languages are primarily spoken.

North America
French
Yiddish

Central America
Spanish

South America
Brazilian
Guarani
Portuguese
Spanish

Caribbean
Dutch
French
Haitian
Jamaican Patois
Spanish

Western Europe
Asturian
Basque
Dutch
Flemish
French
Galician
German
Irish
Italian
Lombard
Spanish
Welsh

Northern Europe
Danish
Estonian
Finnish
Icelandic
Latvian
Lithuanian
Norwegian
Swedish

Central Europe
Czech
German
Hungarian
Slovak

Eastern Europe
Azerbaijani
Belarusian
Georgian
Kazakh
Moldovan
Polish
Russian
Serbian
Ukrainian
Yiddish

**Southern/
Mediterranean
Europe**
Catalan
French
Galician
Greek
Italian
Ladino
Lombard
Maltese
Spanish

**Southeastern
Europe**
Albanian
Bulgarian
Greek
Macedonian
Romanian
Serbian
Slovenian

**Western
Africa**
Akan
French
Hausa

Igbo
Yoruba

**Northern
Africa**
Arabic
French

**Central
Africa**
Bemba
French
Hausa
Kinyarwanda
Kirundi
Swahili

**Eastern
Africa**
Amharic
Arabic
Bemba
French
Kinyarwanda
Kirundi
Oromo
Somali
Swahili
Tigrinya

**Southeastern
Africa**
Chewa
Malagasy
Swahili

**Southern
Africa**
Afrikaans
Swahili
Xhosa
Zulu

**Middle East &
Western Asia**
Arabic
Armenian
Azerbaijani
Farsi
Georgian
Hebrew
Ladino
Oromo
Turkish
Yiddish
(continued)

LANGUAGES BY REGION

Central Asia
Azerbaijani
Farsi
Kazakh
Pashto
Russian
Tajik
Uzbek

Eastern Asia
Cantonese
Hmong
Japanese
Korean
Mandarin
Mongolian
Uzbek

Southern Asia
Bengali
Hindi
Kannada
Nepali
Pashto
Punjabi
Sinhala
Tamil
Urdu

Southeastern Asia
Burmese
Cantonese
Hmong
Indonesian
Javanese
Khmer
Lao
Malay
Sundanese
Tagalog
Thai
Vietnamese

Australia/New Zealand
Maori
Tonga

Micronesia & Polynesia
Marshallese
Tonga